THE SOLDIERS' RECORD
OF
JERICHO, VERMONT

I0182297

E.H. Lane

HERITAGE BOOKS
2007

HERITAGE BOOKS

AN IMPRINT OF HERITAGE BOOKS, INC.

Books, CDs, and more—Worldwide

For our listing of thousands of titles see our website
at
www.HeritageBooks.com

Published 2007 by
HERITAGE BOOKS, INC.
Publishing Division
65 East Main Street
Westminster, Maryland 21157-5026

International Standard Book Number: 978-0-7884-3029-9

SOLDIERS' RECORD.

Sumter has fallen! Nothing, since our existence as a nation, has so thrilled the hearts of the people as this short message, flashed over the wires on that memorable 13th of April, 1861. The alienation and bitterness of the South, which, until now, had only expressed itself in idle threats, had culminated in actual rebellion, and the score of men under the brave and noble Maj. Anderson, which garrisoned Fort Sumter, had been compelled to surrender, not to a foreign foe, but to an enemy of our own household.

For the first time in our nation's history, had the emblem of our freedom and nationality been assailed by an armed rebellion in our midst, and the authority and laws of the Government set at defiance. It instinctively united the loyal people throughout the length and breadth of the North, and party differences were forgotten in the newly awakened patriotism and loyalty of a nation in peril from foes within itself.

The Rebellion must and shall be put down, and the flag of our country, torn down by traitors in Charleston harbor, shall again float over an undivided nation, without a stripe erased or a star stricken out, was the expressed determination of the loyal north in one almost united voice.

On the 15th day of April, 1861, President Lincoln issued a proclamation calling for seventy-five thousand men to serve for three months, to aid in enforcing the laws and suppressing the rebellion—which then gave but faint indications of its subsequent extent and proportions—and made requisition upon the Governor of our State, for its quota of the same. Governor Holbrook immediately ordered all the uniformed militia organized under the laws of the State, to fill up their companies to their full quota, which order was promptly obeyed, and they were organized into the 1st Regiment Vt. Volunteers, and mustered into the service of the United States May 2d, 1861.

In this Regiment, Jericho had three representatives, viz: Abner S. Richardson, Co. A.; Blinn Atchinson and Henry J. Parker, Co. H.

They were mustered out with the Regiment Aug. 15, 1861.

In July, 1861, Congress, assembled in Extra Session, passed an Act authorizing the President to call out 500,000 men, to serve for three years unless sooner discharged.

The work of raising troops, thus authorized, was soon commenced. Under the calls of the President, made by virtue of that Act, the Second, Third, Fourth, Fifth and Sixth Regiments were rapidly organized and sent forward.

The enlistments for these Regiments, from this town, were as follows, viz.:

SAMUEL BENTLEY, age 18, enlisted Aug. 27, 1861, in Co. K. Fifth Regiment; was taken prisoner May 5th, 1864; was paroled, and mustered out March 31st, 1865.

NAPOLEON BISSONETTE, age 20, enlisted Aug. 26th, 1861, in Co. K. Fifth Regiment; was elected Corporal, and was discharged Nov. 26, 1862, for deafness, caused by exposure, and for which he receives a small pension from Government.

JAMES AUSTIN BIXBY, age 18, enlisted Sept. 9th, 1861, in Co. I. Fifth Regiment as private, was promoted Corporal, then Sergeant, and to 2nd Lieut. March 25th, 1863; was wounded June 4th, 1864, and was mustered out Sept. 15, 1864.

EDGAR CHAMBERLAIN, age 18, enlisted Aug. 27th, 1861, in Co. K. Fifth Regiment, was promoted Corporal; re-enlisted Dec. 15th, 1863, and was killed in action near Spottsylvania, May 10th, 1864.

PATRICK DOWNS, age 20, enlisted Aug. 21st, 1861, in Co. K. Fifth Regiment; was promoted Corporal; re-enlisted for Essex Dec. 15th, 1863; was wounded May 6th, 1864; transferred to Vet. Reserve Corps Feb. 21st, 1865, and was mustered out April 27th, 1865.

SIMEON C. EDWARDS, age 28, enlisted Aug. 19th, 1861, in Co. K. Fifth Regiment, and deserted April 14th, 1862.

JOSEPH W. ELLIS, age 18, enlisted Aug. 26th, 1861, in Co. K. Fifth Regiment; was wounded in hip May 5th, 1864, and was mustered out Sept. 15th, 1864. A full pension has been granted him.

TRUMAN C. HATCH, age 18, enlisted Aug. 26th, 1861, in Co. K. Fifth Regiment, and was discharged Oct. 29th, 1862, on account of disability, but enlisted again under a subsequent call.

ALLEN KIMTON, age 24, enlisted Aug. 29th, 1861, in Co. K· Fifth Regiment, and was discharged Jan. 20th, 1863.

CHARLES LUCIA, age 22, enlisted Aug. 21st, 1861, in Co. K. Fifth Regiment; was wounded at Savage Station June 29th, 1862, and taken prisoner; was exchanged July 26th, 1862, and discharged the 29th of September following on account of wounds, and for which a pension has been granted him.

PATRICK LAVELLE, age 18, enlisted Aug. 26th, 1861, in Co. K. Fifth Regiment; re-enlisted Dec. 15th, 1863; was wounded and in hospital May 10th, 1864, and was mustered out June 14th, 1865.

JOHN McGOVEN, age 19, enlisted Aug. 23d, 1861, in Co. K. Fifth Regiment; was wounded and in hospital May 10th, 1864, and was mustered out Sept. 16th, 1864.

DANIEL B. SMITH, age 18, enlisted Aug. 17th, 1861, in Co. K. Fifth Regiment, and was discharged Aug. 26th, 1862. He was wounded in his right hand at Savage Station.

JOHN W. WADE, age 32, enlisted Aug. 22d, 1861, in Co. K. Fifth Regiment, and was discharged Feb. 11th, 1863, having lost an arm in the service of his country.

JASON P. WARE, age 26, enlisted Aug. 31st, 1861, in Co. K. Fifth Regiment, and died at Annapolis, July 21st, 1862, from wounds received in action.

ROBERT WHITE, age 24, enlisted Sept. 6, 1861, in Co. I. Fifth Regiment, re-enlisted for Burlington Dec. 15th, 1863, and was mustered out June 29th, 1865.

In September, 1861, Col. Lemuel B. Platt received orders from the War Department to recruit and organize a Regiment of Cavalry, to serve for three years. The novelty of Cavalry service was attractive to many, and the Regiment was speedily raised, and was mustered into the service of the United States Nov. 19th, 1861. If the idea that this mode of service was easy, induced any to enlist, that idea was soon dispelled.

A position in its ranks proved to be one of constant activity, hardship and danger.

The enlistments in this Regiment, from Jericho, were as follows, viz:

BLINN ATCHINSON, age 21, enlisted Sept. 29th, 1861, in Co. A.; re-enlisted Dec. 31st, 1863, was promoted 1st Sergeant July 15th, 1864, and was mustered out June 21st, 1865. He went out with the First Regiment, thus serving during the entire war. He was wounded in skirmish on picket, March 2d, 1863, in left thigh, by a pistol ball, which has not been extracted, and for which he receives a small pension from Government.

WM. J. FLOWERS, age 27, enlisted Sept. 25th, 1861, in Co. A., and was discharged Jan. 6th, 1863, on account of injuries received in Banks' retreat, but enlisted again under a subsequent call.

EDSON C. HILTON, age 21, enlisted Oct. 16th, 1861, in Co. E. His horse was shot under him in Banks' retreat, and in his fall he was fatally injured. He was discharged Dec. 31st, 1862, and died Feb. 7th, 1863, from the injuries thus received. A pension has been granted to his family.

MARCUS HOSKINS, age 28, enlisted Sept. 30th, 1861, in Co. E., and was discharged Dec. 13th, 1862. He afterwards enlisted in Massachusetts on a call for men for one hundred days, and also for the Frontier Cavalry.

WAREHAM N. PIERCE, age 23, enlisted Dec. 7th, 1861, in Co. A., and was discharged Dec. 26th, 1862, on account of disability. He had previously served in the 12th New York Regiment, that went out under the first call for three months.

The work of raising troops, authorized by Act of Congress in July, still went on. Under it, the Seventh and Eighth Regiments of Infantry, the First and Second Batteries of Light Artillery, and the First, Second and Third Companies of Sharp Shooters were raised.

The enlistments from Jericho in these organizations, were as follows, viz.

FRANKLIN J. BROWN, age 33, enlisted Jan. 4th, 1862, in Co. A. Seventh Regiment; re-enlisted Feb. 17th, 1864, and was mustered out March 14th, 1866.

WILLIAM A. BROWN, age 40, enlisted Jan. 13th, 1862, in Co. A. Seventh Regiment, and died at New Orleans Aug. 13th, 1862. A pension has been granted his family.

DANIEL G. BURNS, age 37, enlisted Dec. 7th, 1861, in Co. A.
Seventh Regiment; was elected Corporal,
and died at New Orleans, Aug. 22nd, 1862.
His family receive a pension.

HIRAM B. FISH, age 25, enlisted Jan. 14th, 1862, in Co. A.
Seventh Regiment; was elected 2nd Lieut.,
and resigned Oct. 15th, 1862, on account
of sickness. A pension has been granted
him for disease contracted while in service,
from which he has not yet recovered.

FREDERICK A. FULLER, age 19, enlisted Jan. 17th, 1862, in
Co. E. Seventh Regiment; re-enlisted Feb.
16th, 1864, and was mustered out March
14th, 1866, serving nearly through the
entire war.

WILLIAM JOHNSON, age 21, enlisted Dec. 7th, 1861, in Co. A.
Seventh Regiment, was promoted Corporal
Oct. 23d, 1862 ; re-enlisted Feb. 20th, 1864,
promoted Sergeant July 16th, 1864, and
was mustered out March 14th, 1866, having served nearly through the whole war.

JOHN H. JOHNSON, age 25, enlisted Nov. 4th, 1861, in 2nd
Co. Sharp Shooters, was promoted Cor-
poral; re-enlisted Dec. 21st, 1863, and was
discharged Mar. 24th, 1864, on account of
sickness. He lived only a week after
reaching home, and died April 6th, 1864.

SAMUEL B. LOCKLIN, age 23, enlisted Oct. 30th, 1861, in 2nd
Co. Sharp Shooters, and was discharged
Dec. 30th, 1862.

MICHAEL F. MARTIN, age 37, enlisted Dec. 5th, 1861, in Co.
A. Seventh Regiment, and was discharged
Oct. 10th, 1862, for disability, for which
he receives a small pension.

ABNER S. RICHARDSON, age 22, enlisted Nov. 21st, 1861, in
Co. A. Seventh Regiment, was elected Ser-
geant, and was discharged Nov. 25th, 1862,
for disability. He had previously served a
three months term of enlistment in the
First Regiment.

BURTON C. RICHARDSON, age 19, enlisted Oct. 31st, 1861, in
2nd Co. Sharp Shooters, was discharged
the November following; but enlisted
again under a subsequent call.

LOREN T. RICHARDSON, age 24, enlisted Nov. 25th, 1861, in
Co. A. Seventh Regiment, and was muster-
ed out Aug. 30th, 1864.

JAMES WHITE, age 21, enlisted Dec. 12th, 1861, in Co. A.
Seventh Regiment, and died at Camp
Williams, La., Sept. 15th, 1862. His
mother received a pension from Government while she lived.

EDWARD C. WHITNEY, age 44, enlisted Oct. 30th, 1861, in
2nd Co. Sharp Shooters, and was discharged
Oct. 15th, 1862, for disability. He afterwards entered the service again.

On the 1st of January, 1862, men were detailed from the
Regiments in the field to act as recruiting officers, and to enlist men to fill up those Regiments.

The men enlisted for that purpose, from Jericho, were as
follows, viz:

EDWIN H. FASSETT, age 18, enlisted Feb. 26th, 1862, in Co. E.
Second Regiment, and was mustered out
Feb. 27, 1865.

NELSON FASSETT, age 37, enlisted Feb. 26, 1862, in Co. E. Second Regiment; re-enlisted April 19th, 1864; was promoted Sergeant Oct. 18th, 1864; Reg. Q. M. Sergt. Feb. 7th, 1865; 1st Lieut., June 18th, 1865, and was mustered out July 15th, 1865.

TIMOTHY KENNEDY, age 40, enlisted March 13th, 1862, in Co. K. Fifth Regiment, and was killed in action June 29th, 1862. His wife receives a pension from Government.

HORACE C. NASH, age 38, enlisted March 11th, 1862, in Co. G. Second Regiment; wounded at White Oak Swamp; was transferred to the Reg. Army, and died at Nashville, Tenn., Aug. 13th, 1864. A pension has been granted to his family.

On the 3d day of April, 1862, the War Department directed that all further recruiting should cease.

So universal had been the unanimity and enthusiasm of the people in sustaining the Government in its efforts to suppress the Rebellion, and so promptly had they responded to the calls for men, that there were thousands in the ranks, more than had been asked for. But this proved to be only a temporary lull in the storm of war, which was soon to break forth with redoubled energy and fierceness, and the cessation in the work of raising men, was of brief duration.

On the 21st day of May following, the Governor was directed to raise one Regiment of Infantry, to be ready in thirty days. An order was immediately issued to raise the Ninth Regiment, and notwithstanding the entire machinery of recruiting had been laid aside, within forty days from the time the first man enlisted, the Regiment was in Camp at Brattleboro.

In this Regiment two men enlisted from this town, viz:

EDWARD B. RUSSELL, age 20, enlisted June 4th, 1862, in Co. F.; was elected Sergeant, but deserted Sept. 30th, 1862.

LEWIS J. WELLS, age 19, enlisted June 27th, 1862, in Co. F., and was discharged Nov. 10th, 1862.

On the first day of July, 1862, the President of the United States issued a call for 300,000 volunteers to serve for three years.

The Governor immediately issued an order for raising the Tenth and Eleventh Regiments. They were raised with great rapidity. Both were full beyond the maximum number required and were in camp at Brattleboro on the 15th day of August.

There were no enlistments from this town in these two Regiments.

Thus far the Regiments had been raised by the State at large, by recruiting officers appointed specially for that purpose, and stationed at the most convenient and accessible points. No particular number of men had been assigned to, or required of each town, as their proportion of the troops to be raised. So general had been the enthusiasm and loyalty of the people of the State, that requisitions for troops were immediately filled, and towns vied with each other in swelling the ranks of the Union Army. Men, from all the avocations and professions of life, promptly responded to their country's call, and thus far, the enlistments had been made without any other bounty than such as Government offered them, and the monthly State pay of seven dollars per month, granted to volunteers early in the war.

But the ranks of the Regiments in the field were becoming rapidly decimated by the casualties incident to the service, and must be filled up. It was decided, that the several towns in the State, should be allowed to raise the necessary number of men in their own way. For this purpose, it became necessary for the first time that each town should have assigned to it, specifically, the number of men it was expected to raise. The quotas of the towns under the call of the President of July 1st, for 300,000 volunteers, were assessed, and the Selectmen were authorized to act as recruiting officers, for the purpose of raising the number of men required, to fill the Regiments in the field.

On the 4th day of August following, (1862), the President made another requisition for 300,000 men, to serve for nine months; and ordered that, if not furnished by volunteer enlistment by the 3d day of September, a draft would be made on that day for the deficiency.

It was at the same time declared by the Secretary of War, that if any State, before the 15th day of August, should not furnish its quota of the call of July 1st, the deficiency would be made up by draft. The time for draft in this State for the three years' men was afterwards extended to Sept. 10th.

Under the call of Aug. 4th, the Twelfth, Thirteenth, Fourteenth, Fifteenth and Sixteenth Regiments of nine months men were organized.

The quotas of our town, as finally fixed, under these calls, were Eighteen three years men, and Twenty-one nine months men.

These men must be furnished in less than thirty days, by voluntary enlistment or by draft. How, and by whom, this imperative call shall be filled, very naturally became the absorbing question. The novelty of the war, which had attracted many at its commencement, was being dispelled, and the magnitude of the Rebellion becoming more clearly understood. The war had become a stern reality, and the ardor and promptness which had manifested itself in filling previous calls, had somewhat abated; but not the patriotism and determination of the people to sustain the Government, and prosecute the war, until a final and complete victory of the Union Army was achieved, and an honorable peace obtained.

A meeting of the tax-payers and citizens was called about the middle of August, and was fully attended. At that meeting, the Selectmen were instructed to offer bounties to those who would enlist to fill the quotas of our town under these calls, and to assess a tax upon the Grand List for the same. It was generally understood that a tax could not be legally voted and collected for this purpose, but the unanimity with which it was voted, gave assurance that most of it would be paid.

A subscription was drawn up, and a sum was readily signed, sufficient to make up such part of the tax as might not be paid. The Legislature, immediately after assembling in October following, authorized towns to raise money for such purposes, and on the 8th day of January following, a town meeting was called, and the tax of seventy cents on the dollar, which had been assessed to pay the bounties under these calls, was legalized, and the collection of it soon completed.

The Selectmen of the town, U. S. Whitcomb, L. A. Bishop and L. L. Lane, immediately entered upon their work with zeal and energy. They offered a bounty of fifty dollars, afterwards increased to sixty dollars, to fill the call for nine months men, and a bounty of one hundred dollars to the three years men; but to complete the quota and save a draft, the last few enlisted were paid a larger bounty.

The men enlisted for nine months' service, all went into Co. F. Thirteenth Regiment, which Company was organized at

Richmond, Sept. 10th, 1862,—which is the official date of their enlistment,—and were as follows, viz:

LUCIUS H. BOSTWICK, age 22, was elected 1st Lieut. of the Company, was promoted Captain March 3d, 1863; resigned June 3d, 1863, on account of sickness from exposure in camp, and died soon after at Washington, of Rheumatic Fever. He was the first to sign the contract of enlistment, and generously offered his town bounty of fifty dollars, and fifty dollars in addition, to the next ten that should enlist. This amount was afterward paid his father, as was also all the money contributed by individuals for bounties.

REUBEN M. BABCOCK, age 19, died Jan. 29th, 1863, at Fairfax, Va., of Typhoid Fever. He was an only son, to whom his parents looked for support, and a pension has been granted them.

WILSON A. BENTLEY, age 21, died at Alexandria, Va., June 25th, 1863, of Typhoid Fever.

ISAAC N. BROOKS, age 18, died at Washington Oct. 28th, 1862, of Typhoid Fever.

ERASTUS POWELL, age 22, died at Occoquan, Va., May 25th, 1863, of Typhoid Pneumonia. He had been examined for admission to the University at Burlington just previous to his enlistment, but leaving the bright prospect of a career of usefulness, gave his services and his life to his country.

CHARLES McCARTY, age 36, was sick in Hospital when the Regiment was mustered out; afterwards discharged, date unknown.

J. T. DREW, not entered on Co. roll.

ELI N. PECK, age 18, was discharged April 6th, 1863, for disability.

2

WILLIS T. WELLS, age 42, was discharged Feb. 2d, 1863, for disability, for which he receives a small pension from Government.

BYRON D. MATTHEWS, age 30, had a finger shot off at Gettysburgh, and was mustered out with Regiment July 21st, 1863.

NORMAN J. RICE, age 33, was elected Sergeant, and mustered out with Regiment.

LOREN T. BENTLEY, age 24, was elected Corporal, and mustered out with Regiment.

JULIUS H. BLISS age 29, was mustered out with Regiment.

MORRIS L. GRIFFIN,	age 20,	do.	do.	do.
NIAL MCGEE,	age 22,	do.	do.	do.
PATRICK MCGOVEN,	age 18,	do.	do.	do.
CALEB P. NASH,	age 18,	do.	do.	do.
BENJ. F. ROBINSON,	age 24,	do.	do.	do.
Z. W. ROCKWOOD,	age 44,	do.	do.	do.
HENRY W. YORK,	age 25,	do.	do.	do.
SAMUEL YORK,	age 22,	do.	do.	do.

The town bounty paid to these men was as follows, viz:

To Lucius H. Bostwick, fifty dollars, as before stated; to Willis T. Wells and Norman J. Rice, eighty-five dollars each; to Julius H. Bliss, Caleb P. Nash and Henry W. York, one hundred and thirty-five dollars each; and to the remaining fifteen, sixty dollars each.

The men who enlisted for three years were as follows, viz:

R. J. THOMSON, age 33, enlisted Aug. 18th, 1862, in Co. A. Cavalry, and died Aug. 7th, 1863, of sun stroke.

DANIEL DIXON, age 19, enlisted Aug. 8th, 1862, in Co. A. Cavalry, and deserted Oct. 30th, 1863.

HUBBELL B. SMITH, age 37, enlisted Aug. 18th, 1862, in Co. K. Fifth Regiment; was promoted Corporal June 1st, 1864, and was discharged Jan. 12th, 1865. He was wounded in the groin by a rifle ball at Winchester, Va., Sept. 19th, 1864, which unfitted him for further active duties in the service, and for which he receives a small pension. He still carries the ball, which has never been extracted, as a memento of the Rebellion.

ZANTHY PARKER, age 45, enlisted Aug. 18th, 1862, in Co. K. Fifth Regiment, and was mustered out June 19th, 1865.

MICHAEL PHILLIPS, age 20, enlisted Aug. 16th, 1862, in Co. L. Cavalry, and was killed in action May 11th, 1864. A pension was granted his widow.

VICTOR LAVALLEE, age 20, enlisted Aug. 30th, 1862, in 2d Co. Sharp Shooters. The only record I have been able to find of him is "dropped from rolls."

JOSEPH RUSSIN, age 32, enlisted Aug. 30th, 1862, in Co. E. Second Regiment and was mustered out June 19th, 1865.

LEWIS TATRO, age 19, enlisted Sept. 6th, 1862, not assigned to any Regiment, and was discharged Nov. 18th, 1862.

JULIUS MILLER, age 27, enlisted Aug. 30th, 1862, in Co. K. Third Regiment, and deserted Nov. 13th, 1862.

The nine men last named, received, each one hundred dollars town bounty.

CHARLES C. RICHARDSON, age 18, enlisted Aug. 22d, 1862, in Co. E. Second Regiment, was missing in action May 12th, 1864, and is supposed to have died in a Rebel prison. Some say he was killed May 5th, 1864, in the battle of the Wilderness. A pension has been granted his father.

ALBERT G. BRADLEY, age 17, enlisted Aug. 12th, 1862, in Co.
H. Second Regiment, was promoted Cor-
poral, and mustered out July 1st, 1865.

CHAUNCEY L. CHURCH, age 21, enlisted Aug. 20th, 1862, in
Co. G. Second Regiment, and was killed
at Banks' Ford, May 4th, 1863. He had
just completed his first year in the Uni-
versity when he enlisted. I cannot better give the manner of
his death, and also a faint idea of the scenes through which
many of our brave boys and men passed, than by copying a
short extract from the biographical sketch, prepared for the
society to which he belonged in college, by one of his com-
rades: "He was in the first battle of Fredricksburg, and
"there fought as only a brave soldier can. In the second bat-
"tle of Fredricksburg, when his regiment charged up the
"hights he again did honor to himself. Although in that
"gallant charge his Regiment lost one hundred and eight
"men in killed and wounded, yet his life was again spared;
"but it was spared for only one short day.

"The next afternoon when the enemy charged upon our
"brigade, he fell while nobly fighting for his country. A rifle
"ball struck him in the forehead, passed through his brain,
"killing him instantly."

ARTEMUS W. BEMIS, age 30, enlisted Aug. 19th, 1862, in 1st
Co. Sharp Shooters, was promoted Cor-
poral, transferred to 2d Co. S. S. Dec. 23d,
1864, and to Co. G. Fourth Reg. Feb. 25th,
1865, and was mustered out June 19th, 1865.

ELIAS BURNS, age 29, enlisted Aug. 22d, 1862, in Co. E.
Second Regiment, was transferred to Vet.
Reserve Corps, July 1st, 1863, and was
discharged July 31st, 1865.

The five last named, received, each one hundred and ten
dollars town bounty.

JAMES S. HERSON, age 21, enlisted Aug. 30th, 1862, in Co. E. Second Regiment and was discharged Jan. 3d, 1863, for deafness caused by exposure, and for which he receives a small pension.

EDGAR E. WRIGHT, age 26, enlisted Sept. 10th, 1862, in Co. A. Cavalry, and was killed near Leetown Va., Aug. 25th, 1864. A pension has been granted his widow.

The two, last named, received, each one hundred and twenty-five dollars town bounty.

OLIVER LUCIA, age 30, enlisted Aug. 22d, 1862, in Co. E. Second Regiment, and was discharged June 2d, 1865. He was wounded in his thigh, causing his death after his discharge, and for which his family receive a pension from Government.

BARNEY LEDDY, age 21, enlisted Aug. 23d, 1862, in 1st Co. S. S., and was killed in action June 22d, 1864.

The two last named, received, each one hundred and thirty-five dollars town bounty.

This completes the enlistments made in the town in this year—1862.

A Brigade Band, of fifteen men, for the Brigade composed of the old Regiments from this State, was raised and mustered into the U. S. service, May 26th, 1863.

ROLLIN M. CLAPP, age 34, enlisted in this Band April 21st, 1863, and was discharged Oct. 19th, 1864.

On the 3d day of March, 1863, Congress passed an Act for enrolling and calling out the National Forces. This law created the office of Provost Marshal General, with a Deputy Provost Marshal in each Congressional District. Under the Deputy Provost Marshals, an enrollment of those liable to do military duty, between the ages of twenty and forty-five, was made, in two classes. The first class was composed of those between the ages of twenty and thirty-five, including those unmarried up to forty-five. The second class was composed of married men between the ages of thirty-five and forty-five. The second class was not to be drafted until the first class was exhausted. The law further provided, that any person drafted under it, would be discharged by furnishing an acceptable substitute, or by paying a commutation of three hundred dollars.

These two classes were subsequently merged into one, and the provision for the three hundred dollar commutation was stricken out, as it was found, by trial, that the draft yielded more money than men, and although money is one of the sinews of war, it was not the sinew most needed to put down the Rebellion.

Under this law, a draft was made at Burlington in July, 1863, for the Third Congressional District, to fill its quota of a call of the President just made for 300,000 men. The draft was ordered by enrollment districts, composed of two or more towns, and not by towns separately, so that no quota was assigned to each town, or any opportunity given them to fill the call by voluntary enlistment.

The persons drafted from Jericho were as follows, viz:

HAWLEY C. BOOTH,   HENRY M. FIELD,
EDWIN J. GLOYD,   GEORGE HALL,
NATHANIEL JOHNSON, Jr., SYLVESTER TARBOX,
        HOSEA S. WRIGHT,

who paid the commutation of three hundred dollars, each.

DAVID R. BIGELOW,   JOSEPH B. KINGSBURY,
BUEL S. MARTIN,   HIRA A. PERCIVAL,
PHILIP PRIOR,   L. F. WILBUR,

who furnished Substitutes.

A few others were drafted, who were exempted for physical disability.

This was the only draft ordered during the war, without an opportunity being first given to towns to furnish their quotas by enlistment, and the only one made in the State, except in a few towns which failed to furnish their quotas under subsequent calls for men, of which number Jericho was *not* one.

But the Rebellion did not stop. The Seceded States, organized as a nation, with all the machinery of Government, under the name of the Southern Confederacy, with a liberal proportion of the military men of ability educated in the schools of the Government they were attempting to destroy, enlisted under their banner, and with almost every man within their borders, able to bear a part, conscripted into their army; and, added to this, the border Slave States which had not openly seceded, lending largely their aid and sympathy to the unholy cause; the Rebellion had assumed a magnitude, that far exceeded the most extravagant calculations of the Government, or of the loyal people at its commencement. The time of service of the nine months men enlisted the previous year, had expired, and the Regiments in the field had again become reduced, and their ranks must be filled up, and it became evident that more calls for men must be made.

On the 2d day of August, of this year—1863,—the Governor directed the raising of the Seventeenth Regiment of Infantry, and the Third Battery of Light Artillery.

But as no new call for men had yet been made, the raising of these organizations progressed very slowly.

On the 17th day of October, 1863, the President of the United States issued his Proclamation calling for 300,000 volunteers for three years service, and announced that if any Sta should fail to raise its quota, a draft would be made for t deficiency, on the 5th day of January, 1864. This call w to fill the ranks of the Regiments in the field, and the Sele men were again appointed recruiting officers, and charg with the duty of raising the quotas of their respective towı The quota of Jericho under this call was twenty men.

A town meeting was held Dec. 2d, at which the Selectmı were authorized to pay a bounty of not exceeding three hu dred and fifty dollars to each volunteer, who should apply c the quota of the town to be, raised under this call, and assess a tax of not exceeding one hundred and forty cents c the dollar of the Grand List, to pay said bounties.

War meetings, as they were called, were held, and weı largely attended by young and old, male and female, and tl Selectmen, L. A. Bishop, R. M. Galusha and Nathan Benham entered upon their task with commendable zeal and energ and the quota was speedily filled.

The men enlisted were as follows, viz:

BLISS A. ATCHINSON, age 19, enlisted Dec. 4, 1863, in Co. A Cavalry, was promoted Corporal Nov. 1 1864, and was mustered out June 5, 186ȝ

JOHN BENWAY, age 40, enlisted Dec. 22, 1863, in Co. H Ninth Regiment, and was mustered 'ou June 13, 1865.

JOSEPH CAMMEL, age 22, enlisted Dec. 26, 1863, in Co. H Ninth Regiment, and died Nov. 22 1864. His widow receives a pension fron Government.

JAMES CARROLL, age 20, enlisted Dec. 10, 1863, in Co. A Cavalry, was transferred to Co. B. June 21, 1865, and was mustered out Aug 9, 1865.

WILLIAM J. FLOWERS, age 29, enlisted Dec. 3, 1863, in Co. H. Ninth Regiment, and died at Newbern, N. C., Oct. 1, 1864, of Yellow Fever. He had previously served in the Cavalry Regiment. A pension has been granted to his widow and minor children.

JAMES FLYNN, age 18, enlisted Dec. 4, 1863, in Co. H. Ninth Regiment, was transferred to Co. C. June 13, 1865, and was mustered out Dec. 1, 1865.

EDWARD FAY, age 18, enlisted Dec. 14, 1863, in Co. A. Cavalry, was transferred to Co. B. June 21, 1865, and was mustered out Aug. 29, 1865.

JOHN GUYOTTE, age 43, enlisted Dec. 28, 1863, in Co. K. Fifth Regiment, was wounded May 5, 1864, transferred to Vet.Reserve Corps Sept. 1, 1864, date of discharge not known.

JOHN H. HASTINGS, age 18, enlisted Dec. 17, 1863, in Co. I. Third Regiment, and was killed at Petersburg, Va., April 2, 1865.

TRUMAN C. HATCH, age 20, enlisted Dec. 2, 1863, in Co. K. Fifth Regiment, was transferred to Vet. Reserve Corps, May 1, 1865, and died at Washington, July 3, 1865. He had previously served in the same Regiment.

PATRICK McGOVEN, age 18, enlisted Dec. 4, 1863, in Co. H. Ninth Regiment, was transferred to Co. C. June 13, 1865, promoted Corporal Oct. 28, 1865, and was mustered out Dec. 1, 1865. He had previously served in the Thirteenth Regiment his term of enlistment.

BERNARD MCKENNA, age 20, enlisted Dec. 26, 1863, in Co.
A. Cavalry, was transferred to Co. B.
June 21, 1865, and was mustered out
Aug. 9, 1865.

THOMAS H. PALMER, age 43, enlisted Dec. 18, 1863, in Co. H.
Ninth Regiment, was transferred to Co.
C. June 13, 1865, and was mustered out
Dec. 1, 1865.

ALEXANDER PLANT, age 22, enlisted Dec. 15, 1863, in Co. K.
Fifth Regiment, and died of wounds re-
ceived May 5, 1864.

VICTOR PLANT, age 18, enlisted Dec. 17, 1863, in Co. K. Fifth
Regiment; was wounded May 5, 1864,
and was mustered out June 29, 1865.

DANIEL E. SMITH, age 21, enlisted Nov. 22, 1863, in Co. I.
Third Regiment, and was killed at
Charlestown, Va., Aug. 21, 1864.

ALEXANDER SPOONER, age 18, enlisted Oct. 29, 1863, in Co.
D. Eleventh Regiment, and was dis-
charged April 9, 1864.

JAMES SWEENEY, age 27, enlisted Dec. 17, 1863, in Co. A.
Cavalry, and was mustered out June 14,
1865.

JAMES HENRY VANCOR, age 18, enlisted Dec. 18, 1863, in Co.
H. Ninth Regiment, promoted Corporal
March 3, 1865, transferred to Co. C. June
13, 1865, promoted Sergeant June 15,
1865, to 1st Sergeant Aug. 8, 1865, to
2d Lieut. Nov. 17, 1865, and was mustered out Dec. 6, 1865.

LEWIS S. WHITCOMB, age 36, enlisted Dec. 28, 1863, in Co. H. Ninth Regiment, was transferred to Co. C. June 13, 1865, and was mustered out Sept. 11, 1865.

The twenty men enlisted to fill this quota were paid each, three hundred and fifty dollars town bounty.

On the 1st day of February, 1864, the President of the United States ordered that a draft for 500,000 men to serve for three years, or during the war, should be made on the 10th day of March, following, unless previously furnished by enlistment. As explained, this was equivalent to a new call for 200,000 men, as the enlistments made under the call of Oct. 17, 1863, were to be deducted from it. The quota of our town under this new call was eleven, and was already filled by credits for reënlistments in the field, which were not reported to the Adjutant General in season to apply on our quota, under the call of Oct. 17, and by enlistments in the Seventeenth Regiment, made while we were filling that quota, but which were not allowed to apply on it, as that call was specially for men to fill the ranks of the old regiments in the field. No men being required of this town under this new call, no town bounty was, nor has since been voted, for the men that filled this quota. They were as follows, viz:

SOLOMON BINGHAM, age 18, enlisted Dec. 21, 1863, in Co. B. Seventeenth Regiment, and was killed while marching near Petersburg, Va., June 16, '64, by a ball fired by an unseen enemy.

BIRNEY W. HILTON, age 18, enlisted Dec. 30, 1863, in Co. B. Seventeenth Regiment, and was mustered out July 14, 1865. He was wounded May 6, 1864, in the neck, by a rifle ball, which has not been extracted. He receives a small pension from Government.

EBEN C. LEMON, age 18, enlisted Dec. 2, 1863, in Co. B. Seventeenth Regiment, was elected Corporal, and was mustered out July 14, 1865.

BURTON C. RICHARDSON, age 18, enlisted Nov. 13, 1863, in Co. B. Seventeenth Regiment, and was mustered out July 3, 1865. He had previously served a short term in the Second Sharp Shooters.

EDGAR CHAMBERLAIN,	re-enlisted	Dec. 15, 1863,	in the field.
BLINN ATCHINSON,	do.	Dec. 31, 1863,	do.
JOHN HIRAM JOHNSON,	do.	Dec. 21, 1863,	do.
PATRICK LAVELLE,	do.	Dec. 15, 1863,	do.
EDWIN H. TRICK,	do.	Dec. 15, 1863,	do.

The soldier last named, enlisted from Burlington Sept. 9, 1861, in Company I. Fifth Regiment, was promoted Reg. Com. Sergeant, and was mustered out June 29, 1865. He was assigned to Jericho, as he claims, by mistake when he reënlisted, and unfortunately for him, applied on a quota for which no town bounty was voted.

The remaining two of our quota was filled by a credit allowed us, as our proportion of a number of men who had been enlisted to the credit of the State at large, having no residence in any particular town.

On the 14th day of March, 1864, the President made another call for 200,000 men, and ordered that a draft be made on the 15th day of April, following, to fill the quotas of such towns as might be deficient. This call was made for the purpose of equalizing the result of the draft, made in July, 1863, by districts, and of raising any deficiency that might exist, in the number of men furnished by any town, under it.

For the first time, under this call, each town was credited with the number of men actually drafted from it. Our quota, and deficiency under all previous calls, was twelve, and the credit of the thirteen men drafted filled it, and gave us one surplus to apply on a future call.

On the 9th day of March, 1864, General U. S. Grant was appointed to the command of the entire Union forces, and the whole power of the Government pledged to his support in crushing the Rebellion. It became evident that the patriotism and loyalty of the North was to be further largely taxed in furnishing men to fill up the ranks of the Union army.

On the 23d day of May, 1864, a circular was issued by the Adj. and Ins. General of the State, in accordance with advices received from the War Department, earnestly urging the towns in the State to commence the enlisting of men at once, in anticipation of another call.

On the 18th day of June, 1864, a town meeting was called, and it was voted that the Selectmen be authorized to pay bounties to volunteers, in anticipation of a call.

This proposition met with some opposition, but was passed by only twenty-three nays. Those who opposed it, did so, mainly from doubts about the expediency of the policy of paying town bounties, and of the ability of the town to continue the policy under all future calls that were likely to be made, and not from any sympathy with the Rebellion, or any disposition to withhold from the Government any needed support.

The Selectmen were authorized to borrow, for the time being, such an amount of money as might be necessary, on the credit of the town; the amount of bounty to be paid was left to their discretion, and they were instructed to enlist, if possible, volunteers at once.

On the 18th day of July, as anticipated, the President of the United States issued a call for 500,000 men, and ordered that a draft be made on the 5th day of September, unless the men should be previously furnished by voluntary enlistment. Under this call men were accepted for one, two or three years, and men enrolled, and liable to draft, were also allowed to furnish substitutes in advance of a draft, thus exempting themselves for the time for which their substitutes were enlisted.

The quota of the town under this call was twenty-three. I cannot better indicate the obstacles which presented themselves in filling this call, than by copying from the Adj. and Ins. General's Report for this year. In it he says, "the recruiting "under this call commenced at a very unfavorable season, "when farmers were in the midst of their most pressing work, "and labor was scarce, and commanding prices hitherto un- "precedented in the State. The very unusual number of "casualties resulting from the pending campaign, which "brought desolation and mourning into many households in "almost every town in the State, also had a very natural ten- "dency to disincline men to enlist, at a time when it seemed "almost inevitable, that if they did so, they would be at once "forwarded to the front, and exposed to the hazard of battle. "But these, and all other obstacles, proved of no avail as "against the loyal determination of the citizens of the State "to respond to the call of the President, at all hazards, and "regardless of expense."

The Selectmen for this year, were Julius Hapgood, George A. Chapman and W. R. Macomber, who entered upon the work of raising the quota with energy and determination, and aided in their efforts by many of our citizens, it was speedily filled.

The men enlisted were as follows, viz:

GILBERT E. DAVIS, age 21, enlisted Aug. 11, 1864, for three years, in Co. I. Fifth Regiment, and was killed at Cedar Creek, Oct. 19, 1864.

MORTIMER W. BROWN, enlisted in August, for three years, in the Twelfth U. S. Infantry. As no reports were made from the Reg. Army to the Adj. Gen., I am not able to give any further record of his service or fate.

CHARLES BENWAY, age 39, enlisted August 11, 1864, for one year in Co. A. Seventeenth Regiment; was taken prisoner Sept. 30, 1864, and it is supposed died.

WILLIAM J. FULLER, age 21, enlisted September 5, 1864, for one year in Co. E. Seventh Regiment, and was mustered out June 6, 1865.

FRANKLIN MARTIN, age 22, enlisted Aug. 17, 1864, for one year, in Co. A. Seventeenth Regiment; was taken prisoner Sept. 30, 1864, was liberated at or near the close of the war, and reached home to be mustered out with his Regiment, July 23, 1865.

LEWIS PERRIZO, age 25, enlisted Aug. 2, 1864, for one year, in Co. K. Fifth Regiment; was slightly wounded, and was mustered out June 19, 1865.

OSCAR J. PIXLEY, age 18, enlisted Aug. 16, 1864, for one year, in Co. A. Seventeenth Regiment; was taken prisoner Sept. 30, 1864, and died at Salisbury, N. C., Jan. 15, 1865.

GEORGE D. SHERMAN, age 20, enlisted Sept. 2, 1864, for one year, in Co. H. Ninth Regiment, and was mustered out June 13, 1865.

CHARLES SWEENEY, age 24, enlisted Aug. 29, 1864, for one year ; not assigned to Regiment, and was discharged Oct. 11, 1864.

RUSSELL TOMLINSON, age 21, enlisted Aug. 12, 1864, for one year, in Co. K. Fifth Regiment, and was mustered out June 19, 1865. He had previously served in the same Regiment, having enlisted for Bolton, Aug. 30, 1861.

LEWIS J. WELLS, age 21, enlisted Aug. 17, 1864, for one year, not assigned, and was discharged Sept. 24, 1864.

JOEL P. WOODWORTH, age 40, enlisted Aug. 31, 1864, for one year, not assigned, and was mustered out May 22, 1865.

BYRON B. HATCH, age 18, enlisted Feb. 2, 1864, in the field, for three years, in Co. K. Fifth Regiment, and died Sept. 29, 1864, in Hospital at Burlington.

WILLIAM JOHNSON, re-enlisted March 14, 1864, in the field.

FRANKLIN J. BROWN, do. March 14, 1864, do.

FREDERICK A. FULLER, do. March 14, 1864, do.

These men were paid a town bounty of five hundred dollars each, except Charles Benway, who received four hundred and fifteen dollars, and Lewis J. Wells, who received four hundred and fifty dollars.

The following persons, enrolled, furnished substitutes to apply on this quota, viz: L. A. Bishop, Daniel B. Bishop, Truman B. Barney, Henry M. Brown, Buel H. Day and Edgar H. Lane, who were each paid four hundred dollars.

The Selectmen also made a deposit of three thousand dollars to the credit of the State Treasurer, under an act of Congress, authorizing recruiting in the Seceded States, and the remaining recruit needed to fill the quota, was thus obtained, at a cost to the town of four hundred and twenty-eight dollars.

On the 6th day of September, 1864, a town meeting was held, and a tax of two hundred cents on the dollar of the Grand List, was voted to pay said bounties.

On the 19th day of December, 1864, the President of the United States made another call for 300,000 men, to be furnished by the 15th day of February, 1865, and ordered a draft on that day, for any deficiency which might then exist.

A town meeting was again called, at which the Selectmen were authorized to pay bounties to fill the quota under this call; the amount of bounty to be left to their discretion, and a tax of one hundred cents on the dollar of the List was voted, to be assessed immediately.

Men were accepted for one, two or three years, but the towns were assured, that it was for their ultimate interest to enlist as many men for three years as possible; as, in assessing future quotas, the years of service furnished, instead of the number of men, was to be the basis of assessment.

Under this call, two companies, the First and Second, were raised in this State for the First Regiment of Frontier Cavalry. These companies were mustered into the service January 10, 1865, and were mustered out June 27, 1865.

The work of recruiting had become extremely difficult. The competition between towns was great, some of which were offering extravagant bounties, and men were enlisted wherever they could be found.

The Selectmen immediately entered upon the work, and before the time the draft was ordered, the quota of the town which, as then understood, was twelve, was filled. The men enlisted were as follows, viz: 3

GEORGE B. DRURY, enlisted Dec. 14, 1864, for three years, in
Co. E. 59th U. S. Colored Infantry; was
commissioned Second Lieutenant, and was
mustered out January 31, 1866.

ROBERT BAXTER, age 31, enlisted Feb. 4, 1865, for three years,
in Co. H. Sixth Regiment, and was mus-
tered out June 26, 1865.

THOMAS H. ERELY, age 21, enlisted Jan. 12, 1865, for three
years, in Co. C. Eighth Regiment, and
was mustered out June 28, 1865.

NAPOLEON LAROSE, age 18, enlisted Jan. 23, 1865, for three
years, in Co. A. Fifth Regiment, and was
mustered out June 29, 1865.

JOHN VAN ORNUM, age 21, enlisted Jan. 10, 1865, for three
years, in Co. E. Fifth Regiment, and was
mustered out June 25, 1865.

These men were paid a town bounty of eight hundred dollars each, except Robert Baxter, who received eight hundred
and fifty dollars.

LEWIS ALBERT, enlisted Jan. 10, 1865, for one year, and deserted two days after.

PETER ALBERT, age 19, enlisted Jan. 10, 1865, for one year, in
Co. F. Eighth Regiment, and was mus-
tered out June 28, 1865.

ROYCE CAMP, age 18, enlisted Jan. 10, 1865, for one year, in
First Company Frontier Cavalry, and was
mustered out June 27, 1865.

JOSEPH PLOOF, age 34, enlisted Jan. 10, 1865, for one year, in
Co. F. Eighth Regiment, and was mus-
tered out June 28, 1865.

LOUIS RICHARDS, age 22, enlisted Jan. 11, 1865, for one year;
not assigned, and was discharged Feb. 10,
1865.

ALFRED HILL, age 30, enlisted Jan. 9, 1865, for one year, in First Company Frontier Cavalry; was promoted Corporal June 1, 1865, and was mustered out June 27, 1865.

BYRON S. HALL, age 19, enlisted Feb. 13, 1865, for one year, in Co. E. Seventh Regiment, and died May 30, 1865.

The men enlisted for one year were paid a town bounty of five hundred dollars each, except Peter Albert and Joseph Ploof, who received five hundred and fifty dollars each.

This was the last call made, and closes the record of enlistments. The number of men furnished by this town during the war, was one hundred and thirty-eight. Eight of these enlisted again, after being discharged or mustered out, and eight reënlisted in the field, making the terms of service one hundred and fifty-four, not including the seven men who were drafted and paid commutation. Of this number, ninety-four were paid a town bounty.

Of the men whose names are herein recorded, ten were killed, and twenty-two died from wounds or disease. Most of these sleep among strangers or on the battle-field, a few have found a resting place among their kindred at home. Of the living, several bear upon their persons, the evidences of their valor, and of their participation in the deadly conflicts of war. Some are suffering from disease contracted in the service, and some have passed unscathed through all the perils of camp and field. Most of them have won for themselves an honorable name, and through this Record, their townsmen tender their gratitude to the living, and their sympathy to the mourning friends of the dead.

The amount of money expended by the town, for bounties and attending expenses, was thirty thousand eighty-four dollars. The taxes voted and assessed, for this purpose, were as follows, viz : seventy cents on the dollar of the Grand List of 1862; one hundred and forty cents on the dollar of the Grand List of 1863 ; three hundred cents on the dollar of the Grand List of 1864; and sixty cents on the dollar of the Grand List of 1865, voted at the annual March meeting—making, in all, five hundred and seventy cents on the dollar of the Grand List of the town, and raising a sum equivalent to a little more than eighteen dollars for each man, woman and child in the town, according to the Census of 1860.

The taxes thus assessed were promptly and cheerfully paid, and almost as soon as the war closed, the last town indebtedness for bounties was extinguished, and the money, in most cases justly and dearly earned, has enabled, in part, many of the soldiers to provide for themselves or their parents, comfortable homes.

Added to this, the patriotic and liberal efforts of the ladies of the town, in collecting and sending forward, every article, which only the ingenuity and sympathy of woman can devise, to add to the comfort and alleviate the sufferings of the sick and wounded soldier, deserves honorable mention, in this Record.

The Medical Department of the army was taxed to its utmost, and could hardly supply the most common wants of the sick and wounded. The articles most needed in the hospitals, and the delicacies necessary for the comfort and cure of its inmates, were, in great part, supplied by the contributions and labors of the people at home.

In procuring and preparing these, the ladies took the lead. Nor were those of our own town behind, in responding to the appeal made to their sympathy and generosity, by these wants of the suffering soldier.

Collectors were appointed, and money, or such articles as were needed, were solicited, and almost every family, rich or poor, contributed something. Meetings and social gatherings were held, and these contributions were prepared in the manner thought to be most useful and convenient, and several boxes were thus filled and sent forward, mostly through the Sanitary or Christian Commissions.

The value of these contributions is not known, as no record of them was preserved.

This noble work, carried on, willingly and cheerfully, asking for no reward, except such as deeds of love and charity always bring, was the means of saving thousands of lives, and alleviating an untold amount of the sufferings of those who went forth to fight the battles of our country, and the sympathy and care thus generously manifested, did much to dispel the dread of enlistment, and to cheer the hearts of the soldiers on to final victory.

The last year of the war was one of unusual activity and severity. Large and repeated calls for men were made ; recruiting was prosecuted on a gigantic scale ; men were enlisted in great numbers and immediately sent forward to serve in the ranks of already the largest army ever put into the field in so short a time. Under the fertile military genius of General Grant, the whole Union army was put in motion. It had become apparent, that the entire military strength of the so-called Confederacy was already in the ranks of their army, and entrenched in a few strongholds on the borders of their territory.

While the eastern division of the army, under the personal command of Gen. Grant, was moving against the rebel hosts under Gen. Lee, strongly entrenched in, and around Richmond, the rebel capital, Gen. Sherman, with the western division of the army, on the 2d day of September, captured Atlanta, the south-western stronghold of the rebellion, and leaving it in ruins, on the 11th day of November, started on his brilliant and triumphal march through the heart of the Confederacy. About the same time Hood's army was defeated and totally routed at Nashville by the Union army under Gen. Thomas. Meanwhile Gen. Grant continued his operations against the army under Gen. Lee, and after a series of battles among the most determined and sanguinary of the entire war, on the 3d day of April, 1865, Richmond was evacuated, followed on the 9th day of April by the surrender of Gen. Lee and his whole army, and on the 26th of April by the surrender of Gen. Johnston with the remaining rebel forces.

Thus ended the bloodiest and most gigantic Civil War which history has ever recorded, and with it passed away that curse of our country, and the cause of the war—American Slavery.

Let us hope that all those pernicious doctrines, the outgrowth of the system of Slavery, which led to the secession of so many States of our Union, have also passed away, and that, in their place, will grow up the doctrine, that human rights are paramount to the rights of States, and that the Declaration of Independence, nobly written by our forefathers, but only in part, adopted by them, will become a full and practical reality.

Let us hope that the bitterness of strife may pass away and soon be forgotten, that harmony and fraternal feeling, between the North and South, may be speedily restored, and the bonds of union again cemented, upon the enduring basis of universal freedom.

Let us also hope, that an overruling Providence has been leading us through this long and bloody contest between oppression and liberty, up to a higher life and a nobler mission as a nation, and that He will give us wisdom to re-construct anew a government, whose nature and office shall be, to elevate, educate, christianize and qualify, and make freemen, truly, of all, of whatever nationality, race or color, whose home shall be within our borders.

If such shall be the crowning results of victory, then shall the noble men who have braved dangers, and suffered hardships in their country's defence, feel rewarded for their sacrifices, and the hearts of those, to whom the war has brought mourning and desolation be cheered by the thought, that their loved ones have not died in vain.

> " And never may they rest unsung,
> While Liberty can find a tongue."

SOLOMON BINGHAM, killed near Petersburg, June 16, 1864.

EDGAR CHAMBERLAIN, killed Spottsylvania, May 10, 1864.

CHAUNCEY L. CHURCH, killed Battle Salem Heights, May 4, 1863.

GILBERT E. DAVIS, killed at Cedar Creek, Oct. 19, 1864.

JOHN H. HASTINGS, killed at Petersburg, Va., April 2, 1865.

TIMOTHY KENNEDY, killed at Savage Station, June 29, 1862.

BARNEY LEDDY, killed Bat. Weldon Railroad, June 22, 1864.

MICHAEL PHILLIPS, killed Bat. of Yellow Tavern, May 11, 1864.

DANIEL E. SMITH, killed at Charlestown, Va., Aug. 21, 1864.

EDGAR E. WRIGHT, killed near Leetown, Va., Aug. 25, 1864.

Killed, 10.

"Twine, Gratitude, a wreath for them,
More deathless than the diadem."

WILLIAM A. BROWN, died at New Orleans, Aug. 13, 1862.
DANIEL G. BURNS, " at New Orleans, Aug. 22, 1862.
LUCIUS H. BOSTWICK, " at Washington, June, 1863.
REUBEN M. BABCOCK, " at Fairfax, Va., Jan. 29, 1863.
WILSON A. BENTLEY, " at Alexandria, June 25, 1863.
ISAAC N. BROOKS, " at Washington, Oct. 28, 1862.
CHARLES BENWAY, " place and date not known.
JOSEPH CAMMEL, " at Governor's Isl'd, N.Y., Nov. 22, 1864.
WILLIAM J. FLOWERS, " at Newbern, N. C., Oct. 1, 1864.
EDSON C. HILTON, " at home. Feb. 7, 1863.
BYRON B. HATCH, " at Burlington, Sept. 29, 1864.
TRUMAN C. HATCH, " at Washington, July 3, 1865.
BYRON S. HALL, " at Mobile, May 30, 1865.
JOHN H. JOHNSON, " at home, April 6, 1864.
HORACE C. NASH, " at Nashville, Tenn., Aug. 13, 1864.
ERASTUS POWELL, " at Occoquan, Va., May 25, 1863.
OSCAR J. PIXLY, " at Salisbury, N. C., June 15, 1865.
ALEXANDER PLANT, " place and date not known.
CHARLES C. RICHARDSON*" supposed in rebel prison, date not known.
R. J. THOMPSON, " near Washington, Aug. 7, 1863.
JASON P. WARE, " at Annapolis, July 21, 1862.
JAMES WHITE, " at Camp Williams, La., Sept. 15, 1862.

Died, 22.

---

* Some say Charles C. Richardson was killed May 5, 1864, in Battle of the Wilderness.

I cannot better give an idea of the part taken by our State in the prosecution of the war, than by inserting in these pages, a list of the Vermont organizations raised, the date of mustering into, and out of, the service of the United States, and the number of engagements in which each, or some portion of each, have borne an honorable part, from which a glimpse may be obtained, of the many dangers, through which our brave men have passed upon all these fields of blood. Of the bravery and fidelity of our Vermont troops, nothing further need be said in this Record, than that they have won for themselves and for their State a national reputation, of which we all may be justly proud.

These organizations were as follows:

FIRST REGIMENT.—THREE MONTHS.

Mustered into service May 2, '61.   Mustered out Aug. 15, '61.
In one engagement.
For this Regiment Jericho furnished three men.

SECOND REGIMENT.

Mustered in June 20, '61.   Mustered out July 15, '65.
In twenty-eight engagements.
Jericho furnished ten men.

THIRD REGIMENT.

Mustered in July 16, '61.   Mustered out July 11, '65.
In twenty-eight engagements.
Jericho furnished three men.

FOURTH REGIMENT.
Mustered in September 20, '61.   Mustered out July 13, '65.
In twenty-six engagements.

FIFTH REGIMENT.
Mustered in September 16, '61.   Mustered out June 29, '65.
In twenty-five engagements.
Jericho furnished twenty-nine men.

SIXTH REGIMENT.
Mustered in October 15, '61.   Mustered out June 26, '65.
In twenty-five engagements.
Jericho furnished one man.

SEVENTH REGIMENT.
Mustered in February 12, 62.   Mustered out March 14, 66.
In five engagements.
Jericho furnished twelve men.

EIGHTH REGIMENT.
Mustered in February 18, '62.   Mustered out June 28, '65.
In seven engagements.
Jericho furnished three men.

NINTH REGIMENT.

Mustered in July 9, '62. Mustered out, last four Companies, December 1, '65.

In four engagements.

Jericho furnished eleven men.

TENTH REGIMENT.

Mustered in September 1, '62. Mustered out June 22, '65.

In thirteen engagements.

ELEVENTH REGIMENT.

Mustered in September 1, '62. Mustered out August 25, '65.

In twelve engagements.

Jericho furnished one man.

TWELFTH REGIMENT.—NINE MONTHS.

Mustered in October 4, '62. Mustered out July 14, '63.

THIRTEENTH REGIMENT—NINE MONTHS.

Mustered in October 10, '62. Mustered out July 21, '63.

In one engagement.

Jericho furnished twenty-one men.

FOURTEENTH REGIMENT.—NINE MONTHS.

Mustered in October 21, '62,   Mustered out July 30, '63.

In one engagement.

FIFTEENTH REGIMENT.—NINE MONTHS.

Mustered in October 22, '62.   Mustered out August 5, '63.

SIXTEENTH REGIMENT.—NINE MONTHS.

Mustered in October 23, '62.   Mustered out August 10, '63.

In one engagement.

SEVENTEENTH REGIMENT.

Mustered in by Companies in '64.   Mustered out July 14, '65.

In thirteen engagements.

Jericho furnished seven men.

FIRST REGIMENT CAVALRY.

Mustered in November 19, '61.   Mustered out August 9, '65.

In seventy-three engagements.

Jericho furnished fourteen men.

FIRST COMPANY SHARP SHOOTERS.

Mustered in September 13, '61. Mustered out September 13, '64.
In thirty-seven engagements.

Jericho furnished two men.

SECOND COMPANY SHARP SHOOTERS.

Mustered in November 9, '61. Mustered out Nov. 9, '64.
In twenty-four engagements.

Jericho furnished six men.

---

*THIRD COMPANY SHARP SHOOTERS.

Mustered in December 31, '61. Mustered out December 31, '64.
In twenty-four engagements.

FIRST BATTERY LIGHT ARTILLERY.

Mustered in February 18, '62. Mustered out August 10, '64.
In four engagements.

SECOND BATTERY LIGHT ARTILLERY.

Mustered in Dec. 16 and 24, '61. Mustered out Sept. 20, '64.
In two engagements.

THIRD BATTERY LIGHT ARTILLERY.

Mustered in January 1, '64.   Mustered out June 15, '65.
In four engagements.

FIRST AND SECOND COMP'S FRONTIER CAVALRY.

Mustered in January 10, '65.   Mustered out June 27, '65.
Jericho furnished two men.

FIRST BRIGADE BAND.

Mustered in May 26, '63.   Mustered out June 29, '65.
Jericho furnished one man.

The number of men furnished by our State during the war, not including veterans reënlisted, and drafted men who paid commutation, was 30,306.   The number that were killed, and that died in the service was 5,128.   If we add to this the number of those who were discharged on account of wounds or sickness, only to come home and die among their friends, it would make a probable total loss, by death, of not less than one-fifth of the whole number that enlisted to fight in defence of the Union and the Country they loved so well.

> " The land is holy where they fought,
>   And holy where they fell;
> For by their blood that land was bought,
>   The land they loved so well.
> Then glory to that valiant band,
> The honored Saviours of the land."

furnish the several quotas of our town, the bounties paid, &c., during four years of war, of which this record is mainly made up, reveals nothing of the daily life of the soldier, nothing of the hardships or exposures in camp and on the battle field, nothing of the suffering from wounds or sickness in hospitals, or starvation and death, or worse than death, in the rebel prisons, nothing of the wearisome marches by day or sleepless nights on duty, nothing of the anxieties and forebodings in the midst of hourly perils and dangers; but that the names of those, who have experienced or risked all of these, for our common welfare, might be preserved in grateful remembrance, the preparation of this Record was unanimously voted.

PREFACE.

In compliance with an agreement made with the Selectmen, the following pages, gathered mainly from official records, have been prepared.

In them, I have endeavored to give a correct, but brief record of the honorable part Jericho has borne in the bloody war of the Rebellion, now happily terminated, and the names of the noble men who enlisted for our town, the age, date of enlistment, the organization in which each one served, and the date of discharge or death of each; also the amount of town bounty paid, and to whom paid.

I have also given in these pages, the names and time of service of the several military organizations of our State sent into the field, and the number of engagements in which each has borne an honorable part, although they do not strictly form a part of the war history of our town, thinking they might be of interest to many who may read this Record, and feeling, that while we have reason to feel proud that our town contributed so freely of her noble men to aid in prosecuting the war for the preservation of the national existence, the reputation of our State, second to none, won by our Vermont troops in the field, is a source of pride and gratification to all.

The details of enlistments under the several calls for men, the date of discharge or death of each, the measures taken to at the board are cut this ... for ... 4763, ... it has ... led to and, ... and ... given at ... with some person to pay the taxes therein ... There shall, during five ... hundred copies of this such ... to the ... in the town, and ... received their ... as and ... the publisher of so ... general circulation in said county.

At the session ... assembly held April 30, 1874, it was voted, "..." of ... to the President of St. Johnsbury Academy ... real estate ... cost ... to be expended in road ... im ... on and ... the ... of said real estate in Passumpsic, being one of the most ... and ... of the ... of Danville, without ... ... change ..."

At the annual town meeting, held March 5th, 1867, it was Voted to authorize the Selectmen to agree with some person to prepare a Soldiers' Record, and procure the printing of five hundred copies of the same, at the expense of the town, and report at the next annual March meeting; said Record to be distributed as the town shall then direct.

At the annual town meeting held March 3d, 1868, it was voted, that one copy of the Soldiers' Record, to be prepared, be furnished to each family, and soldier without family, in town, and to soldiers or their families or parents living out of town, who were enlisted to the credit of this town, without charge.

* 9 7 8 0 7 8 8 4 3 0 2 9 9 *